The activities

- The activities in this book are designec to show whether your children are 'ready' to read or are ready for a more difficult reading level. Their wish to read is the best sign of readiness.

- Many skills are involved, but most of them will be mastered unconsciously, just as your children learned to talk without direct teaching. They do not have to be equally good at, for instance, seeing letters distinctly, drawing, copying or telling a story. Success in particular activities should help you to find their strong points.

- The chart on page 32 details some of the skills and the ways these are linked with progress in learning to read.

The stories at Level 4

- The stories at this level are more varied in their settings and have more complex plots. The West Street characters, however, continue to be at the centre of the stories, and thus give children a feeling of security and familiarity.

- There are more legends and traditional stories at this level, some of which are in verse, as it is important that children should relish and enjoy the rhythms and sound patterns of rhymes, even if they do not understand every word.

- The stories begin to go beyond children's everyday experiences by introducing fantasy and life in the past. This will help to extend your child's horizons; you may want to make direct comparisons between your child's experiences and what happens

r ; first iliar ive it

reading it aloud.

- Always sit comfortably with your child, so that both of you can see the book easily.

- Read the story to your child, making it sound as interesting as possible. Encourage your child to participate actively in the reading, to turn over the pages and to become involved in the story and characters.

- If your child seems confident, you may miss out your own first reading. Suggest that you read the story together the first time. Carry your child's reading along with your own, without slowing up or losing fluency or expression. Do this again, but tell your child that you will stop reading when you get a signal (for example a push on the arm), and will start reading again when given another signal. Then say "Do you want to read the story all on your own now?"

- Finish by asking if you should read the whole story again to your child. Then say "Now you might like to go away and read the story to yourself (or to Teddy or a younger brother or sister) when you feel like it."

The activities at Level 4

- The activities need not be completed at once. They are not a test, but will help your child to remember the

1

words and stories and to develop the further skills required for becoming a fluent reader.

The activities are often divided into three parts.

- One part is designed to encourage discussion about the stories, and to link them where possible with the child's own experiences. Encourage your child to predict what will happen and to recall the main events of the story. Change the wording of the story as much as you like and encourage your children to tell you about the story in their own way.

- One part encourages children to look back through the book to find general or specific things in the text or the pictures. The child learns to begin to look at the text itself, and to recognise individual words and letters more precisely. The activities state clearly when you should give a letter its name, and when you should sound it out. The activities also introduce more writing, largely copying from words in the original story. If your children find this too difficult, copy the words onto a piece of paper for them to trace over.

- One part is headed *Things to do* and consists of activities which your child can do without your help. You may have to read the instructions for the activities first. Suggest that your child tries reading them with you, and then reads them back to you without your help. It is not necessary to repeat the original words exactly, but your child should understand what the instructions mean. Then leave your child to carry out the first activity alone.

- If your child wishes to go on to the next activity immediately, this is fine, but don't insist on it. You may find that the instructions have been read and the activity carried out without you knowing it! This is excellent. Always discuss what your child has done, and give plenty of praise and encouragement.

- Your child might like to build up a 'Book of things I have done from my stories'. This would give a sense of achievement and permanence, as well as enabling you to keep a check on development and what has been done.

- When all the activities have been done, encourage your child to read the story again before you move on to another book. Your child should now feel secure with it and enjoy reading to you.

Robot takes a test

by Helen Arnold

Illustrated by Tony Kenyon

A Piccolo Original
In association with Macmillan Education

"Look, Tony," said Anna.
"This is a book about robots.
It tells us what Robby can do."

"What can Robby do?" asked Tony.

"The book says he can
answer questions," said Anna.

"Let's give him a test," said Tony.
"We'll ask him some questions."

"What shall we ask him?" said Anna.

"We'll ask him about shapes,"
said Tony.
"He's a funny shape himself."

9

Anna pressed the knob on Robby's head.
"What's round and tells the time?"
she asked.

"Whirtle-tirtle, whirtle-tirtle. Whirr,"
said Robby Robot.
"A clock," he said.

"What's round and on the front
of my shirt?" asked Tony.

"Whirtle-tirtle, whirtle-tirtle. Whirr.
A button," said Robby Robot.

"What's round and bounces?"
asked Anna.

"Whirtle-tirtle, whirtle-tirtle. Whirr.
A ball," said Robby Robot.
"A ball! A ball! A ball! A ball!"

"Turn him off, turn him off," said Tony.
"He's getting excited.
Let's give him a rest."

"No. Let's ask him some more
questions," said Anna.
She pressed the knob on Robby's head.

"What's long and thin and wiggles?"
asked Tony.

"Whirtle-tirtle, whirtle-tirtle. Whirr.
The sun," said Robby Robot.

"That's not right," said Anna.
"That's wrong, Robby," said Tony.
"Let's try again."

"What's round and shines in the sky?"
asked Anna.

"Whirtle-tirtle, whirtle-tirtle. Whirr.
A worm," said Robby Robot.

24

"He's in a muddle," said Anna.
"Try again Robby."

"Poor Robby," said Anna.
"We'll read the book again to see
what's wrong with him," said Tony.

Things to talk about

1. Can you remember any of the questions that Tony and Anna asked Robby?
   Which questions did Robby get right?
   Which questions did he get wrong?
   Do you think the questions were hard for Robby to answer?

2. Can you find anything round on Robby?
   Can you find anything else that's round in any of the pictures?
   Can you find anything round in our room?

Looking at pictures and words

1. Find all the answers that Robby gave in the story.
Can you draw each of Robby's answers?

2. Can you find the words for the noise that Robby made when
Anna pressed the knob on his head?
Can you count up the times he made this noise in the story?
Which of the words for this noise start with the letter W
Which word starts with the letter t

3. Can you find all the other words in the story which begin
with the letter W
Now find all the other words in the story which begin with the
letter t
Can you read them aloud?

4. Look at these words:

sun button worm clock ball

Which word is the right answer to each of these questions?

What's long and thin and wiggles?
What's round and tells the time?
What's round and shines in the sky?
What's round and bounces?
What's round and does a shirt up?

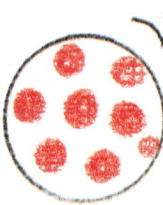